# HEART
# TALK

THE JOURNAL

# HEART TALK

## THE JOURNAL

52 WEEKS OF SELF-LOVE,
SELF-CARE, AND SELF-DISCOVERY

# CLEO WADE

**ATRIA** PAPERBACK
New York ❤ London ❤ Toronto ❤ Sydney ❤ New Delhi

**ATRIA**
PAPERBACK

An Imprint of Simon & Schuster, Inc.
1230 Avenue of the Americas
New York, NY 10020

First Atria Paperback edition September 2020

**ATRIA** PAPERBACK and colophon are trademarks of Simon & Schuster, Inc.

For information about special discounts for bulk purchases, please contact Simon & Schuster Special Sales at 1-866-506-1949 or business@simonandschuster.com.

The Simon & Schuster Speakers Bureau can bring authors to your live event. For more information or to book an event, contact the Simon & Schuster Speakers Bureau at 1-866-248-3049 or visit our website at www.simonspeakers.com.

Manufactured in the United States of America

1 3 5 7 9 10 8 6 4 2

Library of Congress Control Number: 2020942017

ISBN 978-1-9821-4079-3
ISBN 978-1-9821-4080-9 (ebook)

# Contents

# HEART
# TALK

## THE JOURNAL

# Introduction

It has been about two years since *Heart Talk* came out, a book that has truly changed my life.

It is something that has connected me deeply with so many of you and allowed me to be a part of your journey in some of your toughest and most joyous moments.

I am forever grateful to each of you who have let it live with you in your handbag or on a nightstand, and those of you who bought copies for your best friends and your children. Thank you.

I remember when I was writing *Heart Talk* and doing my final read through a couple days before it needed to be sent off to the printers.

As I flipped through it, I had an urge to take out my pen and write some added notes in the margins and underline certain parts of the text.

When I returned the draft to my publisher, I asked that my last-minute additions be put in the book as is—crooked lines and all.

I then edited the introduction to *Heart Talk* to let you know that since I wrote all over my own text, I would love it if you did too.

And just wow.

Over these two years, I have seen the pages of that book ripped out, written all over, highlighted, dog-eared, drawn on, covered in bullet points, doodles, beautiful artwork, poetry of your own, and countless wise reflections from you.

I remember being so scared to put *Heart Talk* out into the world, but you not only accepted it; you made it your own.

This journal is a place for us to continue our collaborations.

I created this to give you more room to discover yourself in our sacred space.

I wrote in *Heart Talk*, "Most people are just looking for a safe space to be themselves," and I know this to be true. I also know what it feels like when *you* have to be the person who must create that safe space for yourself.

Throughout my life, I have found peace and clarity by moving my thoughts, stories, and anxieties out of my body and putting them on paper. Being able to read through my experiences, told *by* me and *to* me, has helped me to deepen my relationship with myself and recognize that I am worthy of self-love, care, and compassion.

This book is designed to be worked through over 52 weeks. Each week has a few words to reflect on, some prompts to help you get started, and a weekly mantra to keep you connected to your practice. As always, with all of my work, there are no real rules. Use the prompts or don't. Do this journal for 52 weeks or 52 days. Draw all over it. Skip weeks and come back to them later. I made this just for you. Engage with it in whatever way feels good to you. All I ask is that you let this book be the place where you are wholly, completely, fiercely, and magically dedicated to YOU. You deserve it.

I love you.
Cleo

THE BEST THING ABOUT YOUR
LIFE IS THAT IT IS CONSTANTLY
IN A STATE OF DESIGN. THIS
MEANS YOU HAVE, AT ALL TIMES,
THE POWER TO REDESIGN IT. MAKE
MOVES, ALLOW SHIFTS, SMILE
MORE, DO MORE, DO LESS, SAY NO,
SAY YES—JUST REMEMBER, WHEN
IT COMES TO YOUR LIFE, YOU ARE
NOT ONLY THE ARTIST BUT THE
MASTERPIECE AS WELL.

# Week 1

I STAY CONNECTED TO MYSELF BY CHECKING
IN ON MYSELF.

When was the last time you slowed down and really checked in on yourself? How are you doing, *really*? Are you okay? Too often we put ourselves last on our list. We make sure everyone in our lives is okay before we check in on ourselves. This journal is about you. It is a space for you to put yourself first. For the first week, we will start with one simple question: How are you? Answer this honestly. How is your work going? Your relationship? How have you been feeling about your family and your friendships? Answer these questions as if someone who loves you and deeply cares about you is asking them, because someone who loves you and deeply cares about you *is* asking you . . . *you.* ❥

*I am . . .*

_____

_____

_____

_____

_____

cleo wade

*I love . . .*

_____

_____

_____

_____

_____

### KEEP GOING

Take the time to be honest. Usually when someone asks us how we are doing, we quickly say "Good!" or "Fine!" Our lives are bigger, deeper, richer, and more complicated than a one-word answer. When we give those answers, we are not truly acknowledging the question. We are not speaking our truth. Dig within. Get honest with yourself. These are the seeds that turn your whole life into a garden of authenticity.

_____

_____

_____

_____

_____

*Lately I have been feeling . . .*

_____

_____

_____

_____

_____

_____

_____

_____

_____

_____

_____

_____

_____

_____

_____

_____

_____

_____

_____

_____

_____

cleo wade

# Week 2

I SHOW MYSELF LOVE BY GIVING MYSELF CARE.

Self-care is a practice designed by you for you, that makes it possible for peace, love, and joy to thrive within you and around you. I use the word practice because true self-care requires work and commitment. It requires us to make healthy choices for our physical and emotional bodies. It also requires us to lighten up, and stop being so damn hard on ourselves. If you are looking to deepen the love you have for yourself, start by learning how to take care of yourself. **If self-love says "I love you," self-care says "prove it."** What do you need to feel cared for? How can you make the time to give yourself care? ᐯ

_____

_____

_____

_____

_____

_____

_____

_____

cleo wade

SELF-CARE IS NOT SOMETHING YOU HAVE; IT IS SOMETHING YOU CLAIM.

## KEEP GOING

What gets in the way of you developing your self-care practice? Remember that self-care doesn't have to cost a fortune; it can be as simple as taking time to breathe deeply, go on a walk, or drink water.

SELF-CARE IS HOW WE
FUEL OUR SELF-LOVE SO
THAT WE ARE ABLE TO
SHARE OUR LOVE WITH
EVERYONE AROUND US.

## owned by you alone

your peace
belongs to you alone
only you
can give it
to yourself
and only you
can take it away

# Week 3

MY PEACE BELONGS TO ME AND ME ALONE.

Sometimes when the world feels hectic or we get annoyed with someone or something, we feel robbed of our peace. Know that nothing can truly take your peace away, and if you feel you have lost it, it is always available for you to reclaim. What brings you peace? What gives you peace of mind? Share it on these pages, and visit your peaceful thoughts whenever you need a reminder. They have the power to act as life rafts when the waters of the world feel like they are rising above our heads. 🌱

*I feel peace when . . .*

_____

_____

_____

_____

_____

_____

## KEEP GOING

Find your peace within. Peace cannot be shared or created with others if you cannot first generate it within.

cleo wade

# Week 4

KNOWING MY NEEDS IS A SUPERPOWER.

Our world often tells us there is something wrong with needing something or someone, or that expressing our needs is somehow a sign of weakness. This is completely untrue. Knowing our needs is a limitless superpower that can help us make all of the big decisions in life. Be unapologetic when it comes to your needs. They are, at the very least, deserving of being seen and heard. What are your needs? Create a list of them, and spend this week planning how you will make space for them in your life. For example, if you need more time for yourself, commit to waking up thirty minutes earlier than you usually do to sit with yourself while having your morning coffee. 𝓦

*From myself I need . . .*

_____

_____

_____

_____

_____

_____

*From my friends & family I need . . .*

_____

_____

_____

_____

_____

_____

_____

_____

_____

_____

_____

_____

_____

_____

_____

_____

_____

_____

_____

_____

*Romantically I need . . .*
   \* When we know what we need from a partner, we spend much
   less time dating the wrong people.

*In my work I need . . .*

   \* When we know what we need to feel challenged & motivated
   by our work, we are much more in tune with what we want
   our career path to look like.

_____

_____

_____

_____

_____

_____

_____

_____

_____

_____

_____

_____

_____

_____

_____

_____

_____

_____

_____

# Week 5

I AM GRATEFUL FOR CHANGE BECAUSE IT
EMPOWERS MY PERSONAL GROWTH.

When we fear change, it keeps us in an energy of feeling stuck, powerless, and resentful. When we embrace change, we open ourselves to endless opportunities and possibilities. Personal happiness is born from personal growth, and personal growth is not possible without a willingness to change. Spend this week reflecting on change. When has change been challenging for you? When has it felt good? How have you changed in the past year? In the past five years? What have you learned from your growth? Change can be hard and uncomfortable at times, but it is necessary. It is also important. And if we let it, it can make life exciting. 𝒱

cleo wade

## it's only natural

of course
I've changed,
darling . . .
I've grown.

## KEEP GOING

What changes would you like to make today? This month? This year? Life is not supposed to stay the same; we are not supposed to stay the same. Our life, our communities, and our world are always in bloom.

## all of it

which parts of yourself won't you let yourself
love yet?

befriend your ingredients

the spicy, the sweet, the pain, the heartache, the gifts, the shame,
and the shine

fall
in love
with
*all*
of you

savor
yourself

# Week 6

I DESERVE TO FALL IN LOVE WITH ALL OF ME.

We ignore so much of who we are, forgetting that we cannot love ourselves wholly if we cannot see ourselves wholly. Can you open up, take an honest look at yourself, and, regardless of what you find, send love there? What parts of yourself have yet to be loved by you? Are there things about your personality that make you feel insecure or self-conscious? Are you silly? Can you love yourself at your silly moments? Are you shy or loud? Can you love yourself when those parts of you are present? Spend this week falling in love with all of you. Enjoy who you are. 🌱

*I love myself because I am . . .*

_____

_____

_____

_____

_____

_____

_____

_____

_____

_____

_____

_____

_____

_____

_____

_____

_____

_____

_____

_____

cleo wade

*I love myself even when I am . . .*

_____

_____

_____

_____

_____

_____

_____

_____

_____

_____

_____

_____

_____

_____

_____

_____

_____

_____

_____

_____

_____

# Week 7

MY CONFIDENCE COMES FROM REMEMBERING
THAT I AM ENOUGH. THERE IS NOT ANOTHER ME
IN THE WHOLE WORLD. I AM RARE, UNIQUE,
AND BEAUTIFUL.

Confidence is not something we have; it is something we practice so that it lives in flow with all that we do. Like most other things, confidence doesn't run on one big gesture. We don't have it by saying to ourselves, "Okay, today I am going to be confident." True confidence starts with affirming ourselves regularly and treating ourselves kindly. Does your mental chatter prop you up? Does it remind you that you are capable of whatever you wish to accomplish? If it doesn't, can you practice choosing new thoughts? Use these pages to nourish yourself with confident and supportive words. Can you compliment yourself three times a day every day this week? Build yourself up and approach your life with the vibrancy of "I got this!" because at the end of the day, who is to say you don't? 🌱

cleo wade

## DAY 1

1. I am . . .

2. I am . . .

3. I am . . .

## DAY 2

1. I am . . .

2. I am . . .

3. I am . . .

## DAY 3

1. I am . . .

2. I am . . .

3. I am . . .

## DAY 4

1. *I am* . . .

_____

2. *I am* . . .

_____

3. *I am* . . .

_____

## DAY 5

1. *I am* . . .

_____

2. *I am* . . .

_____

3. *I am* . . .

_____

## DAY 6

1. *I am* . . .

_____

2. *I am* . . .

_____

3. *I am* . . .

_____

**DAY 7**

1. I am . . .

_____

2. I am . . .

_____

3. I am . . .

_____

*When I combat my negative self-talk with positive affirmation, I notice . . .*

_____

_____

_____

_____

_____

_____

_____

_____

_____

_____

_____

MAY ALL OF
YOUR VIBES SAY:

I GOT THIS

# Week 8

THESE TOUGH FEELINGS ARE NOT ME. THEY ARE MOVING THROUGH ME AND CAN LEAVE OUT THE SAME DOOR THEY CAME IN.

No matter how much work we do on ourselves, stress and anxiety will still find ways of showing up. Our job is not to avoid them, it is not to wrestle with them or "cope" with them. These types of emotions are unavoidable visitors. Let us accept them as a part of life. When they come in, acknowledge their arrival, evaluate what invited them in, and recognize that they are guests, not permanent fixtures. We may not be able to control the arrival of tough emotions, but we do have the power to release them. These feelings are not *you*; they are moving through you. If you are feeling overwhelmed by these uncomfortable emotions, pause. Breathe slowly and deliberately, and tell yourself that you are okay. Remember your strength. Dedicate this week to leaving any of these challenging feelings on these pages. Unburden yourself by moving them out of your mind and body. ᐯ

_____

_____

_____

_____

_____

_____

_____

_____

## KEEP GOING

What feelings have you been noticing this week? Remember, we may not always have the power to control what shows up at our door, but we always, always, always have the power to decide what stays and what goes. Negative and harmful feelings have no home within your sacred space. Let them come and let them go.

_____

_____

_____

_____

_____

_____

_____

_____

cleo wade

# Week 9

I LIVE WITH INTENTION. I AM MOTIVATED NOT ONLY BY WINNING THE RACE BUT BY <u>WHY</u> I STARTED RUNNING TO BEGIN WITH.

We often find ourselves where we don't want to be because our goals or sense of self have been hijacked by fear-based opportunity seeking, pressures from others, or self-doubt. To stay connected to our goals during these moments, we can't just know what we want; we have to know why we want it. Living with intention means we know the reason behind our motivations. Are you clear about what guides your decision making? What is your *why*? What are the roots of your desires and the source of your ambitions? Investigate. Knowing why you choose the directions of your life will help you to continuously move forward on your path. ❦

_____

_____

_____

_____

_____

WHAT IS YOUR
WHY?

WHAT MAKES
YOU WANT
WHAT YOU
WANT?

## KEEP GOING

Our intention is our internal compass. What direction is yours pointing you in?

cleo wade

# love never lies

shame never tells
the truth
it tells you
you are not
good enough
the truth is
you are
it tells you
you have to be perfect
the truth is
you don't
it tells you
your mistakes
are fatal wounds
the truth is
you heal
it tells you
everything has fallen apart
the truth is
you will rebuild
it tells you
that you will stay sunken in despair
the truth is
you will rise

# Week 10

I AM LETTING GO OF SHAME. IT WILL NOT ADD
A SINGLE SMILE, DOLLAR, OR MINUTE TO
MY LIFE.

Shame is a familiar face that pretends to be a friend. It is a discomfort that somehow lives in our comfort zones. The true nature of your life and all the possibilities within it will never be found through the veil of shame. Release shame. Replace it with self-compassion, self-kindness, and self-love. These are your true friends on your precious journey. When have you felt shame? When has it gotten in the way of your ability to feel belonging, enough-ness, and love? ᭡

_____

_____

_____

_____

_____

_____

_____

## KEEP GOING

You are okay. You belong. You are lovable. No matter what happens, know that you are always deserving of love. When we disconnect with our lovability, we disconnect with our ability to heal.

# Week 11

NOT EVERY GROUND IS A BATTLEGROUND. I AM
WORTHY OF SAFE SPACES DEDICATED TO PUTTING
MY MIND AND BODY AT EASE.

Let yourself relax. The wise soldier knows that not every ground is a battleground. While there are many things we must fight for, we cannot live every day in the trenches. To live in a state that requires you to constantly be prepared to go to battle is exhausting. No human body or soul can sustain that type of energy as a lifestyle. Take a moment to assess your energy. Is it tense? Jumpy? Are you in attack mode? Has defensiveness become a way of life? What causes this tension within you? Where is it coming from? What makes you feel calm? Can you gift yourself time to relax each day this week, even if it is just a five-minute walk around the block or ten long, deep breaths at work? Remember that the ground is not only a place where we march toward what we must fight for; it is also a place where we are being divinely held up by the earth. 🌱

*My battleground feels like . . .*

_____

_____

_____

_____

_____

_____

_____

_____

_____

_____

_____

_____

_____

_____

_____

_____

_____

_____

_____

_____

_____

_____

*My holy ground feels like . . .*

_____

_____

_____

_____

_____

_____

_____

_____

_____

_____

_____

_____

_____

_____

_____

_____

_____

_____

_____

_____

_____

When do you feel rested? For example, a friend of mine once said to me, "I feel rested when I slow down and don't let the pace of the world become my pace."

# Week 12

## GRATITUDE IS A CELEBRATION I AM ALWAYS INVITED TO.

I saw a sign in my hometown one day that said, "Until further notice . . . celebrate everything." I have kept that in my heart as a daily mantra because it exemplifies the simplicity of gratitude. Often we think gratitude is a big, complicated idea, but it is simple. It is a thank-you to everything and everyone supporting you to be in your story as it unfolds. Saying thank-you is easy. Fill these pages with thank-you notes. It could be to an elementary school teacher, someone who was nice to you at the grocery store, your partner, a friend. Let this week be a thank-you party, and notice the joy that the spirit of gratitude brings. 🌱

_____

_____

_____

_____

_____

_____

THANK
YOU!

_____

_____

_____

_____

_____

_____

_____

_____

_____

_____

_____

_____

_____

_____

_____

_____

_____

_____

_____

_____

_____

_____

_____

_____

THANK YOU!

_____

_____

_____

_____

_____

_____

_____

_____

_____

---

**KEEP GOING**

To be thankful is to be in conversation with all of life's blessings.

---

_____

_____

_____

_____

_____

_____

_____

_____

_____

THANK YOU!

cleo wade

THANK YOU!

THANK YOU!

# Week 13

SOMETIMES THE BEST PRESENT IS TO

BE PRESENT.

To be present is to bring your total awareness and undivided attention to the moment you are currently in. When was the last time you were truly present? Between our wandering minds and our phone's ability to instantly transport us to the online world, it has become increasingly difficult to just *be where we are.*

How can you practice staying in the moment? When have you been truly present and felt the benefits of being in the moment? Is there a relationship in your life that is suffering from a lack of presence on your part? How can you change that? We can know the gifts that lie in the present only if we stay in it long enough to receive them. ✌

*I struggle to find myself present when . . .*

_____

_____

_____

_____

cleo wade

*I have felt most present when . . .*

_____

_____

_____

_____

_____

_____

_____

_____

_____

_____

_____

_____

_____

_____

_____

_____

_____

_____

_____

_____

cleo wade

*A few things I can do to be more present . . .*

Are there any rituals
in your life, like sitting
down at the dinner
table each night, that
you can make phone-
free zones?

# Week 14

MY JOY IS A GIFT THAT I AM ALWAYS WORTHY OF RECEIVING.

Often when the world feels chaotic, we begin to feel as if it is somehow inappropriate to have joy. Have your joy. Joy is a form of radical self-care. We need it, especially during challenging times, because it is the most revitalizing force within us. Rain or shine, joy is a spiritual energy within us that says, *I will define the current state of the world around me; it does not define me.* What brings you joy? Whether it is dancing, singing to yourself, or letting yourself laugh, find your joy, even if only for a moment. This week, fill these pages with moments of joy. Who brings you joy in your life? What activities add joy? When do you feel most connected to joy? ⚘

*I find joy when I . . .*

_____

_____

_____

_____

_____

cleo wade

*I find joy when I am with . . .*

_____

_____

_____

_____

_____

_____

_____

_____

_____

_____

_____

_____

_____

_____

_____

_____

_____

_____

_____

_____

cleo wade

*Even on my hardest day, these things bring me joy:*

_____

_____

_____

_____

_____

_____

_____

_____

_____

_____

_____

_____

_____

_____

_____

_____

_____

_____

_____

_____

# Week 15

MY EGO IS IN ME, BUT IT IS NOT ME. THE BEST
OF WHO I AM HAS ROOM TO SHINE WHEN MY EGO
IS NOT BLOCKING MY LIGHT.

We all know what it feels like when our ego creeps in: we act vain, jealous, stubborn, overly competitive, and/or defensive (to name just a few!). When we behave this way, it is so important to remember that this is not your true self. An ego builds in all of us as a result of our fears or painful experiences. We may not be able to rid ourselves of the ego entirely, but we can certainly stop it from trying to run our lives. Try to notice when your ego is doing the talking, making decisions about your life, or stepping its muddy foot all over your relationships. When you start to become aware of its presence, you will find it easier to pause, regroup, and put the real you back in charge. When do you feel that your ego comes out the most? Who in your life triggers your ego to flare up? What do you think fuels your ego? 🌱

*When my ego is present I feel . . .*

---

## KEEP GOING

The spirit is never holding us back from an attitude
adjustment, only the ego does that.

*When my ego is not present I feel . . .*

_____

_____

_____

_____

_____

_____

_____

_____

_____

_____

_____

_____

_____

_____

_____

_____

_____

_____

_____

_____

# Week 16

I SHOW LOVE FOR MYSELF BY SURROUNDING
MYSELF WITH PEOPLE WHO DESERVE MY MAGIC.

One of the chief ways we show ourselves love is by surrounding ourselves with loving people. When we love ourselves, we respect the sacred space we take up in the world. No one who sucks your energy, puts you down, makes you feel small, or is unloving to you is entitled to your time. How do the people in your life make you feel? Is there anyone around you who is not showing you the good love you deserve? Is there anyone who makes you feel insecure rather than secure? In what ways can you create space from the people who make you feel this way? No one, no matter who it is, deserves to make you feel bad about yourself: not a parent, not a partner, not an employer, not a friend, not a family member. No one. Hold on to this truth as you fill these pages. ✌

### KEEP GOING

We sometimes stay in friendships & relationships based on how people used to treat us, not how they currently treat us. Are there any people in your life whose kindness is only found in memories?

## a release

I am holding on
but
my hands are tired
and
turning red
this had me thinking
maybe to love
I had to
let go
instead

# Week 17

I LET GO AND ALLOW WHAT IS MEANT FOR
ME TO STAY AND WHAT IS NOT MEANT
FOR ME TO GO.

What are you holding on to? Is it taking all of your energy? Are your hands clenched? Is your body tight? Is your soul strained? Sometimes when something is important to us, we try to control it by attaching heavy stress, worry, and anxiety to it. Whether it is in a relationship with a romantic partner, a family member, or someone at work, if it feels forced, imbalanced, and unhealthy, ask yourself why you are holding on to it so tightly. Can you try to loosen your grip? Take a deep breath, and as you exhale, consider what it would feel like to mentally or emotionally detach from this person or situation. Letting go is a part of life. It is not always easy, but learning to do it is what allows us to peacefully move forward in our lives. ⋎

*It is time to let go of . . .*

_____

_____

_____

cleo wade

LET WHAT IS MEANT TO BE . . . BE. WHAT IS MEANT FOR US FLOWS FREELY IN HARMONY WITH US, NOT AGAINST US.

Love yourself enough to walk into only the rooms and situations that show care and love for you.

Love yourself enough to walk out of the rooms that harm you in any way.

Love yourself enough to hold the people who harm you accountable for their words and actions.

Love yourself enough to express your wants, your needs, and your desires.

Love yourself enough to tell the truth.

Love yourself enough to say enough is enough when enough has become enough.

A LOVE LIKE THIS MOVES MOUNTAINS.

# Week 18

MY BOUNDARIES ALLOW ME TO LOVE MYSELF
AND OTHERS AT THE SAME TIME.

Boundaries mean that we move through the world loving others without betraying the love we have for ourselves. They help us claim the space we need to keep ourselves safe and sane. It can be difficult to create boundaries because they require us to speak up or leave situations that other people want us to stay in. You deserve to be seen, heard, safe, and respected. Are there relationships or spaces in your life where these qualities are not present? Where do you lack boundaries? Clear boundaries are the support beams that hold up healthy relationships. They make it possible for equality and reciprocity to be the driving forces in our relationships with our loved ones, colleagues, and neighbors. ❦

_____

_____

_____

_____

_____

## KEEP GOING

If you are scared to set a boundary by saying something to someone about how you feel and requesting different behavior from that person, ask yourself why you would let any person or thing take up space in your life in a way that does not allow you to show yourself big, good, and deliberate love.

cleo wade

# be heard

sing your song

if that is what
is inside of you
sing
your
damn
song

do
your soul
that
favor

# Week 19

I AM NOT WAITING FOR ANYONE ELSE TO TELL
ME WHO I AM. I GIVE <u>MYSELF</u> PERMISSION TO BE
WHO I WANT TO BE.

No one knows us better than we know ourselves. You don't have to wait for anyone else to give you permission to be who you are or who you want to be. If you want to be a singer, be a singer. Think like a singer, say you are a singer, and, of course, sing your song. *Authorize yourself.* Take charge of your life in this way. What are you calling a hobby that is actually your passion or your purpose? What are you not allowing to be a part of your identity because it is not yet financially lucrative? Be everything you want to be. You are here for a reason. Do not be afraid to take up space in the world that is uniquely yours. ⚘

cleo wade

CHOOSE YOU.
BE YOU.
LOVE YOU.

## KEEP GOING

When I was writing *Heart Talk*, I had a day job at the
same time that helped me pay my rent. Even though
I went into an office every day that had nothing to do
with my book, I never allowed that job to make me feel
that I wasn't a writer. I knew in my heart that as long as
I was writing, I was a writer. What title have you yet to
claim in your journey?

# Week 20

KIND THOUGHTS, KIND VIBE, KIND LIFE.

You are the first person you speak to in the morning. What does that you sound like? Are you trash talking yourself *to yourself*? Are you celebrating yourself? Are you creating nervous chatter? How you speak to yourself sets the tone for how the rest of the world will speak to you; use that power to lift yourself up and create your standard for loving communication. The best and easiest way to combat negative self-talk is by creating a self-kindness practice. Begin yours this week by writing down one thing about yourself each day that you are proud of. Our world needs more cheerleaders. Start by being one for yourself. ⋎

## DAY 1

*Today I am proud of myself for:*

_____

*because . . .*

## DAY 2

*Today I am proud of myself for:*

_____

*because . . .*

## DAY 3

*Today I am proud of myself for:*

_____

*because . . .*

## DAY 4

*Today I am proud of myself for:*

_____

*because . . .*

## DAY 5

*Today I am proud of myself for:*

_____

*because . . .*

## DAY 6

*Today I am proud of myself for:*

_____

*because . . .*

# DAY 7

*Today I am proud of myself for:*

_____

*because . . .*

*When I practice self-kindness I find . . .*

_____

_____

_____

_____

_____

_____

_____

_____

_____

_____

_____

# Week 21

I KNOW MY VALUE. I HONOR MY VALUE. I SPEAK
UP FOR MY VALUE.

Know the value of knowing your value. Do you know what you are good at? Are you in touch with your gifts and talents? When you go to work, do you know what you bring to the table? Some of the best advice I ever received was from my first mentor at my first real job in New York City: "Don't wait for anyone to tell you what you are worth. You have to be the first person who *knows* what you are worth and can *say* what you are worth." What are your time and energy worth in your professional life and your personal life? Get to know your value, and learn how to express it. Knowing it deep within you makes sharing it with others much easier and less scary. ❦

*Some of my talents, skills, and gifts are . . .*

_____

_____

_____

_____

_____

## KEEP GOING

In the world of work, you have to be the first one who knows the value of your talents and also the first one who can express what you are worth to your boss, client, or collaborator. Similarly, in the world of dating and relationships, you have to be the first one to tell another person how your time and energy deserve to be repeated.

*My talents, skills, and gifts are worthy of . . .*

KNOW THE
VALUE OF KNOWING
YOUR VALUE.

# Week 22

I HANDLE MY TRANSITIONS WITH GRACE,
REMEMBERING THAT THEY ARE A TEMPORARY AND
NECESSARY PART OF MY JOURNEY.

Very few breakthroughs come without a few breakdowns along the way. Stay the course. Our personal evolution brings so much brilliance to our life, but it can also bring some pain and discomfort. Transitional periods can be an emotional roller coaster. Be gentle with yourself. Moving from where you were to where you are takes some getting used to. Are you moving through a period of transition? Or, have you gone through one recently that was tough? Reflect on how you feel or felt during these times. What did you learn? ⋎

## KEEP GOING

Growth is not always comfortable. Remember, we call it "growing pains," not "growing pleasures." It may not be easy, but you can get through this.

# I did not lose the lesson

I did a lot of things
not in the right way
some may even call them
mistakes

I just call them
the scars
that keep me
from touching the oven
too long
when it is hot

# Week 23

I RELEASE REGRET AND MOVE FORWARD
WITH THE KNOWLEDGE AND WISDOM
I GAIN FROM MY EXPERIENCES.

Life does not always hand us the easy road or always allow us to be in the right frame of mind to do the right thing at the right time. To know this is to remember that we are human. No one is born knowing the best way to navigate the worst circumstances. I once heard someone say that regret is simply when you are spending too much time focusing on decisions you made while you were still learning. Where in your life are you spending too much time obsessing over a decision you made in your past? Where do you feel that regret overwhelms your ability to move forward? Always remember, our lives are bigger than a single mistake. 🌱

---

---

---

---

## KEEP GOING

We are all more than our mistakes. We are all more than who we were yesterday. Choose to allow what you go through to fuel your growth rather than stunt it. What have you been calling "regret" that was actually a life lesson? What did you learn from it?

# how to keep going

pause
breathe
repair your universe
proceed

# Week 24

WHEN I TAKE TIME TO REPLENISH MY ENERGY,
I HAVE MORE TO GIVE TO MYSELF AND THOSE
AROUND ME.

Do you make space in your life to replenish your energy? Our lives often get so busy and demanding that we run ourselves down to the point of exhaustion. One of the most critical ways we give ourselves care is by knowing what helps restore our energy and sense of self. What helps you do this? Alone time? Movies and Chinese food at home in your pajamas? Spending an extra fifteen minutes in bed cuddling with a pet or a loved one? An hour of yoga or stretching in the morning? If you feel that you are running on empty, pause and take time to fill your tank. Start by figuring out what fuels your joy and energy. ⋎

*Things that help me recharge . . .*

_____

_____

_____

_____

_____

## KEEP GOING

Do you feel the difference between moving through your day exhausted vs. energized? What are some things you notice when you are overtired? What stops you from taking the time to recharge?

MAYBE DON'T DO THINGS

THE WAY YOU HAVE

ALWAYS DONE THEM

SIMPLY BECAUSE THAT

IS THE WAY YOU HAVE

ALWAYS DONE THEM.

# Week 25

I AM OPEN TO BEING FLEXIBLE. I DO NOT HAVE
TO DO THINGS THE WAY I HAVE ALWAYS DONE
THEM SIMPLY BECAUSE THAT IS THE WAY I HAVE
ALWAYS DONE THEM.

There can be no flow in your life without the spirit of flexibility. When we walk into situations feeling so sure of who we are and what we know, we are unable to create space for others or for our own personal growth. Do you allow yourself to be flexible? Or do you feel yourself being tense and strict? To be "in flow" means that you are able to move through the world with the ability to roll with whatever comes your way. Check in on yourself. In what areas of your life do you feel the most rigid or stubborn? Where can you loosen up? We can have discipline in our lives without losing our ability to be spontaneous or try things a different way. 🌱

*I find myself tense when . . .*

> When we are
> flexible, we open
> ourselves up
> to a mountain
> of possibilities,
> new ideas, and
> revelations.

cleo wade

*I think I could be more flexible by . . .*

_____

_____

_____

_____

_____

_____

_____

_____

_____

_____

_____

_____

_____

_____

_____

_____

_____

_____

_____

# Week 26

I AM MORE THAN MY WORST THOUGHTS AND I RELEASE THEM BECAUSE THEY DO NOT SERVE MY HIGHEST SELF.

This week, we are doing a purge of our junky, unhelpful thoughts in order to make room for healthy ones. Healthy thinking happens when we choose to guide our thoughts in a way that benefits our best self and life. We become the stories we tell ourselves. All of our thoughts, especially our repetitive ones, manifest themselves in our lives. Healthy thinking does not mean we never have dark thoughts; it just means that we don't allow them to live and grow within us to the point where they have the power to influence our reality. Dump those thoughts. Break up with them on these pages. Banish them from your being. And if you want to, at the end of the week, rip these pages out and shred or *safely* set them on fire. You don't need them. ❦

*The following thoughts, stories, and ideas no longer serve me . . .*

_____

_____

_____

cleo wade

cleo wade

CLEAN OUT YOUR THOUGHTS BECAUSE THEY HAVE THE POWER TO COVER YOUR ENTIRE LIFE IN DIRT.

YOU WANT LOVE?

BE LOVE.


YOU WANT LIGHT?

BE LIGHT.

cleo wade

# Week 27

I FIND WHAT I AM LOOKING FOR IN THE OUTSIDE
WORLD BY EMBODYING IT WITHIN ME.

When we are in a state of positive and loving energy, the whole room feels it—maybe even the whole world. This week, meditate on what it would be like to wholly embody love. What does it feel like? Warm? Calm? Generous? Steady? Uplifting? Encouraging? What actions show love? Define the energies of love and light for yourself. When we know these energies intimately, they exude from our being, and we are able to detect and attract them in the outside world. ⚡

*When I give love, I feel . . .*

_____

_____

_____

_____

_____

_____

_When I receive love, I feel . . ._

cleo wade

_____

_____

_____

_____

_____

_____

_____

_____

_____

*Light is the best of who we are. What does your light look like in action?*

_____

_____

_____

_____

_____

_____

_____

_____

_____

_____

_____

# Week 28

BECAUSE I AM GRATEFUL FOR WHERE I AM, I
RESPECT THE ROAD THAT GOT ME HERE.

Who we were yesterday is a part of who we are today, whether we like it or not. Can you accept, respect, and forgive your past self? We have all thought, said, or done embarrassing things out of ignorance or immaturity. It is part of growing up and becoming who we are today. Can you make peace with all the phases of your life? What version of yourself do you judge too harshly? Can you love who you were ten years ago? Two years ago? Two days ago? What thoughts, beliefs, or ideas have you outgrown? What life experiences have helped you broaden your point of view? Being fully happy with who we are in the present comes from being okay with our past, not from disregarding it. 𝓥

*I send love and respect to all phases of my life, including . . .*

_____

_____

_____

_____

_____

_____

_____

_____

_____

_____

_____

_____

_____

_____

### KEEP GOING

Can you let where you have been help you appreciate where you are?

_____

_____

_____

_____

_____

_____

_____

_____

_____

# Week 29

I ACHIEVE MY GOALS BY BEING RESILIENT, NOT PERFECT.

The people we admire for exhibiting excellence are not the people who are "perfect" or always seem to succeed. The roads to achieving our goals are paved with victory *and* defeat. Those who are triumphant are celebrated not because they win every time but because they never quit when they lose. When have you missed out on something because you were afraid to try? What is something big you have always wanted to do? When have you tried something but maybe gave up too soon? We all have a fear of failure. Don't let that be what stops you from stepping into your greatness. 🜨

---

cleo wade

### KEEP GOING

You are more resilient than you can imagine. Whatever obstacles you may have faced or are currently dealing with . . . keep going.

cleo wade

DO THE THINGS
THAT SHOW YOU
WHAT YOU ARE
MADE OF.

REMEMBER NOT TO

CARE ABOUT THE THINGS

YOU DON'T EVEN

CARE ABOUT.

# Week 30

I DO NOT INVEST MY TIME, ENERGY, AND THOUGHTS ON PEOPLE, PLACES, OR THINGS THAT AREN'T ACTUALLY IMPORTANT TO ME.

Sometimes our habitual thinking takes over, and we end up being upset about things that don't actually matter to us. The first step in changing a habit like this is to become aware of when we do it. What do you find yourself troubled or annoyed by regularly? Is it actually even important to you? Do you value it enough to exhaust yourself emotionally by putting it on a mental loop in your head? You are in charge of how much space something or someone takes up in your life. Take this week to do an audit. *What are you caring about that you don't actually even care about?* Leave on these pages the irrelevant grievances that you no longer want to be intertwined with your spirit. ⋎

## KEEP GOING

Is there anything taking up precious real estate in your mind that doesn't deserve it? Dismiss what does not serve you.

BE CAREFUL WHEN IT COMES
TO FOCUSING ON THE OPINIONS
OF OTHERS—YOU COULD END
UP WALKING A DAY IN THE
LIFE OF EVERYONE ELSE'S
SHOES BUT YOUR OWN.

cleo wade

# Week 31

I ALLOW FOR THE INFINITE INTELLIGENCE
WITHIN ME TO BE THE GUIDING LIGHT ON
MY JOURNEY.

It is a gift in life to have loving friends, family, and other types of support as a sounding board when we are in crisis or in need of help or advice, but we must remember to balance the opinions of others with our own inner wisdom. No one will ever know your life the way you do. So while it is important to ask for help when we need it and show gratitude for advice from others, we must also know the difference between considering someone's opinion and giving it the power to dictate our own life. What ideas or advice has your inner self been giving you lately? Notice what thoughts and desires are reoccurring in your mind. The more we listen for these messages, the clearer they become. ✔

## KEEP GOING

When do you find yourself struggling to trust your intuition? When have you chosen the opinions of others over listening to your own gut?

DO NOT IGNORE
YOUR INTUITION—
LET IT BE YOUR
GUIDING LIGHT.

# Week 32

I CREATE MY OWN FINISH LINES AND ALLOW
FOR THERE TO BE MANY THROUGHOUT
MY LIFE.

There is no one finish line in life that will leave us completely satisfied. Our lives are made up of a series of goals, achievements, and points of passage that are all connected. Do you feel restless? Are your goals in need of refreshing? Is there a finish line you have been sitting on too long? This week, reflect on what you would like to apply yourself to next so you can tap into the motivation and inspiration that lives within you. ♈

_____

_____

_____

_____

_____

_____

_____

_____

## KEEP GOING

It is important to enjoy our successes, while also remembering that to revolve our lives around one moment of glory or victory does not usually result in sustained happiness. When we consistently reset our goals, they are able to grow with us.

TO KNOW THAT YOU
ARE A WORK IN
PROGRESS MEANS
TO RECOGNIZE
THAT YOUR GOALS
ARE ALSO WORKS IN
PROGRESS.

# what truth will do

and
are we so
scared
that the truth
will hurt us
that we
are willing to
never give it
the opportunity
to
let it
teach us
motivate us
inspire us
heal us
&
maybe
just maybe
free us
too

# Week 33

I AM UNAFRAID OF THE TRUTH, FOR IT GIVES
ME THE CLARITY I NEED TO MOVE FORWARD
WITH MY LIFE.

The best and the worst thing about the truth is that it gets instant results. What truths are you hiding from? When do you find yourself turning away from something and saying, "I don't even want to know"? What things are you pretending not to notice because you are afraid that the truth of the matter will make you uncomfortable? No matter how scary the truth may be, allow it to give you the gift of clarity. Clarity empowers us to move through life on a more focused and deliberate path. 🌱

*Honestly . . .*

## KEEP GOING

Do not let fear of what the truth will reveal keep you from it. Go after it. Let the truth liberate you.

# Week 34

I USE MY LANGUAGE POWERFULLY AND
PURPOSEFULLY.

Complaints have no magic. They don't make anyone's day better and they don't help any situation. Can you commit yourself to going on a complaint cleanse this week? Can you monitor when complaints pop into your mind, and instead of saying them out loud, let them go or write them in this journal? What do you find yourself complaining about too often? At the end of this week, reflect on what you noticed. Did anything surprise you? Did you find you complained more or less than you imagined? ⚡

_____

_____

_____

_____

_____

_____

_____

## KEEP GOING

Keep in mind that there is a difference between complaining (speaking about something negatively in a way that will neither help nor change the situation) and speaking up to bring awareness or attention to something that is not right or fair. A complaint cleanse is not meant to silence you; it is meant to support you by allowing your language to be a more peaceful, deliberate, and magical force.

COMPLAINTS
HAVE NO MAGIC.

## a message from today

maybe
don't
tomorrow
your
life
away

# Week 35

I WILL NOT ALLOW PROCRASTINATION TO DICTATE THE DIRECTION OF MY JOURNEY. I TAKE CHARGE OF MY LIFE BY GETTING SH*T DONE.

The energy of procrastination creates a staleness surrounding our dreams. It delays our destiny and holds our ideas and brilliance hostage. When you work to overcome procrastination, you are able to lead your life rather than be dragged along by it. What do you keep putting off? Write down all the things you want to get done, give yourself a deadline, and then cross each thing out once it is complete. Allow these pages to hold you accountable. It is never too late to become the person you have always wanted to be. Begin today. ♥

*Sometimes I feel stuck because . . .*

_____

_____

_____

_____

_____

_____

_____

_____

_____

_____

_____

_____

_____

_____

*This week I will . . .*

_____

_____

_____

_____

_____

_____

_____

_____

_____

_____

_____

_____

cleo wade

*This month I will . . .*

*This year I will . . .*

_____

_____

_____

_____

_____

_____

_____

_____

_____

_____

_____

_____

_____

_____

_____

_____

_____

_____

_____

_____

cleo wade

*In my precious lifetime I will . . .*

_____
_____
_____
_____
_____
_____
_____
_____
_____
_____
_____
_____
_____
_____
_____
_____
_____
_____
_____
_____
_____

## it was time

so I said yes
I said yes to living
I said yes to loving
I said yes to being
my . . .
self
illuminated
and unafraid

cleo wade

# Week 36

I LOVE MYSELF ENOUGH TO SAY YES TO WHAT
I WANT AND DESERVE.

We are all familiar with the act of standing in our own way. Sometimes it is because we are scared. Maybe you are in the final interview for your dream job, and all of a sudden you start thinking, "Can I really do this?" or you finally meet the romantic partner you know you deserve and you ask yourself, "Am I worthy?" *Yes. You can do it. Yes. You are worthy.* Move out of your own way, say yes to yourself, yes to what you want, and yes to the world. We cannot achieve our goals and desires if we do not have the ability to receive them. What parts of your life are missing a big, juicy YES? What gets between you and yes? Spend this week finding your yeses. ᴡ

*This year, this life, I am saying yes to . . .*

_____

_____

_____

_____

cleo wade

YES! YES! YES!
DON'T JUST SAY YES . . .
CELEBRATE YOUR YES.
IT IS A VICTORY!

# Week 37

I DESERVE MY DREAMS. WHO ELSE COULD THEY POSSIBLY BELONG TO MORE THAN ME?

Every thought, vision, and idea that frequently occurs in our psyche happens for a reason. Our dreams are our destiny's way of communicating with us. Do you believe your dreams are possible? Do you believe you deserve them? More often than not, we spend too much time looking at our dreams through the veil of insecurities and challenges blocking our way. Regardless of what lies between you and your dreams, can you approach them with the energy that says, "*I can, I will, and I am deserving*"? This will not only get you one step closer to attaining them; it will make the journey toward them much more joyful. ⚘

*I dream of . . .*

cleo wade

YOU CAN!

_____
_____
_____
_____
_____
_____
_____
_____
_____
_____
_____
_____
_____
_____
_____
_____
_____
_____
_____
_____
_____
_____
_____
_____
_____

YOU WILL.

cleo wade

YOU ARE
DESERVING.

_____
_____
_____
_____
_____
_____
_____
_____
_____
_____
_____
_____
_____
_____
_____
_____
_____
_____
_____
_____
_____
_____
_____

## as I go forward

I may stumble
but
I stand up
more
than I fall
down

cleo wade

# Week 38

I AM MORE OKAY THAN I THINK.

When we trip and fall, we seem to obsess only over the ten seconds we were on the ground rather than the rest of our day we spent walking perfectly fine. How much of your time do you waste focusing on your missteps? Sometimes we let one heavy moment, month, or year block our ability to see that we are much more okay than we think. Falling down can feel painful or shameful, but it does not define us. Getting up does. Continuing to rise and move forward does. What misstep are you ready to leave behind you? When have you learned from a slip-up? Where can you find gratitude in the moments of your life where you held your balance through challenging times? ᴠ

*Some moments I made it through . . .*

_____

_____

_____

_____

_____

_____

## KEEP GOING

What you got through you can get through.

*Some moments that felt like a big deal at the time but in retrospect were not so bad after all . . .*

---

---

---

---

---

---

---

---

---

---

---

---

---

---

---

---

---

---

---

---

---

---

# Week 39

I APPLY MY WORK ETHIC TO MY WHOLE LIFE.

Our work ethic is something that must be applied to our home, our family, our community, and our world. How can you apply your work ethic to your relationship with yourself and the people around you? It is often so easy to devote ourselves to creating a healthy business. Can we devote that same energy to creating a healthy life? Toni Morrison wrote, "You are not the work you do; you are the person you are." Can you live with ambition for your entire existence? To what area of your life can you bring more of your gifts and talents? 🌱

*Devotion to giving care to myself looks like . . .*

_____

_____

_____

_____

_____

_____

*Devotion to giving care to my loved ones looks like . . .*

_____

_____

_____

_____

_____

_____

_____

_____

_____

_____

_____

_____

_____

_____

_____

_____

_____

_____

_____

_____

cleo wade

*Devotion to giving care to my community looks like . . .*

Every aspect of
your life can be
made better with
your hard work,
love, and devotion.

## these things take time

I am
the caterpillar right now
I may not be flying high
like a butterfly
but
I am
sure as hell

grounded

# Week 40

I APPRECIATE AND ENJOY ALL THE MOMENTS
OF BECOMING WHO I AM.

Divine timing is real. The caterpillar enjoys the energy of being grounded as much as it will enjoy the energy of being a butterfly in the sky. This is because one cannot exist without the other, and every phase of the cycle is equally necessary to the next. Where are you in your journey? Even if you are not exactly where you want to be, can you tell yourself that wherever you are now is okay? The pathway to our destination is where we develop wisdom, strength, and character. Can you find joy and meaning in each step you take? 🦋

_____

_____

_____

_____

_____

_____

_____

ACCEPTING WHERE YOU ARE, HELPS YOU TO LEARN FROM WHERE YOU ARE.

## KEEP GOING

I have found that it is actually the jobs we have before
our dream job that help us figure out what our dream
job even is. This is the same in relationships—our bad
ones help us figure out what a good one looks like.
Where you are today informs where you can be tomorrow.
What is there to learn & enjoy right now?

Everything is
happening on time.
Trust that where
you are is okay.

# Week 41

I AM LOVING AND SUPPORTING MYSELF BECAUSE
I AM MY BEST FRIEND TOO.

Best friends give loving and sound advice. Best friends cheer you on and don't let you beat up on yourself. Best friends support you as you grow and evolve. Best friends show you care and compassion, and they show up for you not just in the big moments when you need it most, but in small, thoughtful, day-to-day ways as well. We seem to always know how to be a best friend to someone else but have a hard time directing that same energy within ourselves. Can you reflect inward and give yourself advice on a troubling situation? Are you able to tell yourself you will be okay when you feel vulnerable? Can you give yourself the same goodness, patience, and support you give your friends? This week, design a healthy friendship with yourself. How would you treat yourself if you were your own best friend? ⱳ

*Best friends deserve . . .*

_____

_____

_____

_____

_____

_____

_____

_____

_____

_____

_____

_____

_____

_____

_____

_____

_____

_____

_____

_____

_____

_____

_____

_____

_____

_____

_____

_____

_____

_____

### KEEP GOING

You are with yourself for as long as you live—how can you get good at being a best friend to yourself?

_____

_____

_____

_____

_____

_____

_____

_____

_____

cleo wade

*Because I am my best friend too I will . . .*

---
---
---
---
---
---
---
---
---
---
---
---
---
---
---
---
---
---
---

# Week 42

## REAL LEADERS LEAD WITH LOVE.

Being a leader means believing in the people around you.

We don't have to embody negative, immoral, or intimidating behavioral traits in an effort to gain respect from others. When we lead with love, we are strong and valuable because of the care, compassion, and empathy we show ourselves and others. Are you currently in a leadership role or aspire to be in one? What type of boss or leader have you admired in the past? What about those leaders made you feel inspired? When has a leader made you feel bad? When have you struggled to respect someone else's leadership style? How can you lead with love? ❧

_____

_____

_____

_____

_____

_____

_____

## KEEP GOING

Part of being a leader is believing in others. You never know if your words of support could be the sign someone is looking for to feel capable of committing to their own greatness. When has someone believed in you? How did it impact you?

YOU WILL
NEVER REGRET
LEADING WITH
LOVE.

## the only battle

I had been
so focused
on winning
and losing
I did not realize
the only battle
was the one
between me and
myself
*for*
myself

# Week 43

MY SENSE OF SELF COMES FROM WHAT I BRING
TO THE WORLD, NOT FROM WHAT THE WORLD
BRINGS TO ME.

When we allow for our wins in life to let us feel that we are on top of the world, we give equal power to allowing our losses to make us feel that the weight of the world is on our shoulders. We can enjoy our successes with less ego and more generosity by remembering that our purpose lies in what we bring to the world, not in the accolades the world brings to us. What are you allowing to define you? How might you be letting the outside world pressure you into uncomfortable feelings about yourself? How can you remain humble and firmly rooted in your sense of self regardless of whether you are experiencing an accomplishment or a disappointment? Know that you are more than an insult, compliment, award, promotion, demotion, divorce, or bad review. ❥

## KEEP GOING

When we release outside pressure, we are more connected to who we really are and what we really want.

cleo wade

# Week 44

GETTING IT OUT IS THE FIRST STEP IN
LETTING IT GO.

Get it out! These pages have been placed here for no other reason but for you to have a space to vent. What has been irritating you lately? What feels overwhelming or stressful? Move this stuff out of your mind and body, and put it in this book. Don't hold it in a minute longer. Put your frustrations on paper, yell into a pillow, dance it out, go for a run, or talk to a friend. Nothing has to stay trapped inside you that you don't want there. 🌱

## brave enough to show up

yell
if you need to

need
if you need to

live
while you
are here

The world does not need your
silence. The world does not
need you to say you are fine
when you aren't.

cleo wade

## with eyes closed

I hold myself tightly and say
I am in this with you
I am here for you
no matter what happens
I will take care of you

doing this
is me
choosing to be on my own team

doing this
is me
learning to hold myself down through even a
hurricane

doing this
is how I am able to
live my life
rather than let
my life
live me

*self-intimacy is self-care, self-care is self-love*

cleo wade

# Week 45

I LEARN HOW TO CARE FOR MYSELF BY MAKING
TIME TO LISTEN TO MYSELF.

Intimacy requires us to listen to ourselves and handle what we hear with care. Do you have an intimate relationship with your thoughts? Do you spend time with yourself, listening to what's going on in your head and heart? Do you care for your feelings by being there for yourself when you need consoling? Do you have an intimate relationship with your body? Do you listen to it when it tells you what foods, language, and movement feel life-affirming? Do you listen when it tells you what substances feel heavy or toxic? Spend this week diving within. Intimacy with ourselves means showing up for all aspects of our being and doing it with trust, gentleness, and care. ❦

*When I listen to my body, it tells me . . .*

_____

_____

_____

_____

_____

cleo wade

*When I listen to my heart, it tells me . . .*

_____

_____

_____

_____

_____

_____

_____

_____

_____

_____

_____

_____

_____

_____

_____

_____

_____

_____

*When I listen to my mind, it tells me . . .*

THOUGHTS

DREAMS

IDEAS

cleo wade

The intimacy you
are searching for
outside yourself
must first be
found within.

# Week 46

MY WISDOM COMES NOT JUST FROM WHAT
I LEARN. IT ALSO COMES FROM WHAT
I UNLEARN.

It is important to keep learning and adding new tools to our toolboxes. That said, while adding more knowledge and information is important, editing ideas and habits from our being is just as useful. As we go through life, we begin to realize how much our experiences and environments are absorbed into our personalities. For example, if we were raised in a home where people yell when they are angry, we are very likely to have learned to express ourselves that same way when angry. The time is always right to unlearn something within us that no longer serves us. What are you ready to unlearn? Which of your current strategies or survival methods could use some editing? When we empower ourselves to unlearn unhealthy behavior, we create more space to learn new and improved ways of being in the world. ⚘

## KEEP GOING

Sometimes how we grow up or where we are from can build bias or inaccurate judgments about others based on things like gender, sexual preference, religion, or skin color. Are there any ideas about others you may be holding consciously or subconsciously that are outdated?

# Week 47

I ACCEPT MY RISKS KNOWING THAT THEY WILL
BENEFIT ME, TEACH ME, OR BOTH.

We often dread risk-taking so much that the mere thought of it immediately fills us with anxiety. Try instead to apply acceptance to risk-taking. Acceptance brings trust and calm into our decision-making processes so we can move forward with more steadiness, confidence, and ease. Whenever I am trying to overcome the fear of taking a risk, I think about this quote from Nelson Mandela: "I never lose. I either win or I learn." When we recognize that all our life experiences offer life lessons, we see that most risks, no matter how they work out, benefit us, teach us, or both. Reflect on your relationship with risk-taking on these pages. ✌

*What risks have you been avoiding? What about them makes you feel anxious or afraid?*

_____

_____

_____

_____

_____

_____

_____

_____

_____

_____

_____

_____

_____

_____

### KEEP GOING

When have you observed (either in your life or someone else's) a risk that either paid off or led to learning a valuable life lesson?

_____

_____

_____

_____

_____

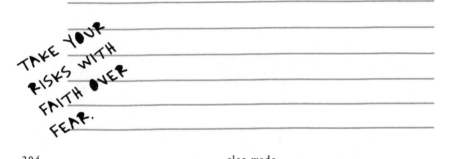

TAKE YOUR RISKS WITH FAITH OVER FEAR.

cleo wade

DON'T JUST
CALCULATE
YOUR RISKS.
FULLY ACCEPT
THEM AS WELL.

# Week 48

THROUGH GRATITUDE, I RELEASE THE ENERGY
OF MORE, MORE, MORE AND REPLACE IT WITH
THE ENERGY OF THANK-YOU, THANK-YOU,
THANK-YOU.

There is almost nothing more important or life-altering than the power of gratitude. Developing a practice of gratitude is not only wise; it is practical. Understanding how to feel grateful for what we have frees us from the uneasy state of constantly wanting and helps us to differentiate between what we want and what we actually need. It also allows us to calm the mind and put less pressure on ourselves, releasing us from the never-ending hunt for more. Each day this week, can you find three things, no matter how big or small, to be grateful for? 🌱

**DAY 1**

*Today I am grateful for . . .*

1.

2.

3.

**DAY 2**

*Today I am grateful for . . .*

1.

2.

3.

**DAY 3**

*Today I am grateful for . . .*

1.

2.

3.

**DAY 4**

*Today I am grateful for . . .*

1.

2.

3.

**DAY 5**

*Today I am grateful for . . .*

1.

2.

3.

**DAY 6**

*Today I am grateful for . . .*

1.

2.

3.

DAY 7

*Today I am grateful for . . .*

1.

2.

3.

*When I stayed connected to gratitude each day, I noticed . . .*

_____

_____

_____

_____

_____

_____

_____

_____

_____

_____

_____

## forgiveness

do not
spend your time
trying to wrap your head
around
the idea of
forgiveness
it is not
intellectual

forgiveness

is spiritual
it is one of the most
spiritual things
we could ever do

# Week 49

I FREE MYSELF BY FORGIVING MYSELF.

Forgive yourself. Forgive yourself for who you were last week, last month, or last year. Forgive yourself for when you were exhausted and snapped at the people you love. Forgive yourself for not being able to "do it all." Forgive yourself for your mistakes. Forgive yourself for the things you should have realized sooner. Forgive yourself for eating one cookie too many. Forgive yourself for not being "perfect." What are you ready to forgive yourself for? Leave all of it on these pages. Self-forgiveness frees us from the prison of anger, shame, judgment, and resentment. Set yourself free, only you have the key to do so. 🖤

## turn the lock

the past
cannot stay
the past
if
it is always
on your
mind
there is
only one
person
holding the
key
that frees you
from the shackles
of
days gone by

*you.*

cleo wade

P.S.: Learning to forgive others starts by truly learning how to forgive yourself.

# a love note to my body

a love note to my body:

first of all,
I want to say
thank you.

for the heart you kept beating
even when it was broken

for every answer you gave me in my gut

for loving me back
even when I didn't know how to love you

for every time you recovered when I pushed you past our
limits

for today,

for waking up.

# Week 50

YOU ARE MY ONLY BODY. I RESPECT YOU. I
APPRECIATE YOU. I LOVE YOU.

Spend this week writing a love note to your body. We spend so much time beating up on and shaming our bodies. Part of living in the light of self-love is being grateful for what you have. Your body is with you your entire life, it is your partner in all things. Send it love. ♥

*Dear Body,*

_____

_____

_____

_____

_____

_____

_____

_____

_____

_____

cleo wade

_____

_____

_____

_____

_____

_____

_____

_____

_____

_____

_____

_____

_____

_____

_____

_____

_____

_____

_____

_____

_Love,_

_____

# what happens to pain

time and time again
my soul
and
my spirit
and
my learning heart
prove to me

*I heal*

## Week 51

THE LOVE IN MY HEART IS MORE THAN THE
PAIN I FEEL WHEN IT BREAKS.

Heartbreak is so incredibly mysterious: while on the one hand, we are in so much pain with amplified feelings of loneliness and abandonment, we are also in an elevated state of sensitivity, allowing us to be hugely in tune to the information our heart has to offer. Have you had your heart broken before? Are you going through heartbreak right now? Whether it is with a lover, a friend (the toughest ones in my opinion!), or a family member, reflect on the experience this week. We can fully tap into all that our emotional intelligence has to offer only when we are able to really sit with what we are feeling, even when we are feeling pain. Try not to avoid the pain too much. There is a certain type of magic that comes through pain, for it is where we learn our power to keep going, no matter what we go through. 🌱

cleo wade

## KEEP GOING

When your heart is in pieces, you have the power to pick up those pieces. You have the power to put your heart back together one piece at a time and build something new.

cleo wade

## strong flower

baby,
you are
the strongest
flower
that ever
grew
remember that
when
the weather
changes

cleo wade

# Week 52

I AM IN BLOOM. I AM IN BLOOM MY WHOLE LIFE.

Know that you are strong. Every living thing on this planet is here with the divine support of Mother Nature. She always has your back. Her support will see you through any weather. The best thing about strength is that when you embody it, you build it and you get stronger. You are growing into exactly who you need to be spiritually, physically, and mentally.

How are you feeling at the completion of this journal? Reflect on the journey you have taken this year, and also take a moment to congratulate yourself for the dedication it takes to complete a year-long journal. (Also, if it took you longer than a year, that's okay, you know there are no rules when it comes to my books!) I love you. I hope this journal has helped you to love you too. 🌱

cleo wade

AND BE SURE TO KEEP YOUR LIGHT

BRIGHT AND SHINING—YOU NEVER

KNOW JUST HOW MANY PEOPLE

YOU MAY BE A LIGHTHOUSE FOR.

YOU NEVER KNOW HOW MANY

PEOPLE FIND THEIR WAY HOME,

IN EVEN THE WILDEST STORMS,

BECAUSE YOU ARE THERE.

*Love, Cleo*